Little People, BIG DREAMS™

LUDWIG VAN BEETHOVEN

Written by
Maria Isabel Sánchez Vegara

Illustrated by
Romina Galotta

Frances Lincoln
Children's Books

Little Ludwig was born in the city of Bonn in Germany. Both his father and grandfather were musicians, and they hoped that Ludwig would follow in their footsteps. But no one could have imagined how far his talent would take him!

His feet could barely reach the floor when he started taking piano lessons from his dad. Soon, Ludwig's little fingers were flying over the keys with ease. But his father was very strict, even waking him to practice at night.

At seven, Ludwig played in front of an audience for the first time and blew them away! Hoping to impress them even more, his dad said he was six. But Ludwig didn't need to pretend—his musical genius spoke for itself.

Five years later, he was writing his own music.
Ludwig composed three beautiful piano pieces. He dreamed
of one day creating music for more instruments, and perhaps
even a symphony, a big piece for a whole orchestra.

To earn some money to support his family, Ludwig worked for years as a musician and piano teacher.

Later, he moved to the city of Vienna, Austria, where he met two famous composers, Haydn and Salieri.

Ludwig was learning from the best, but he didn't want to follow anyone's rules! At his first big concert, he played one of his own pieces. It sounded bold, exciting, and new.

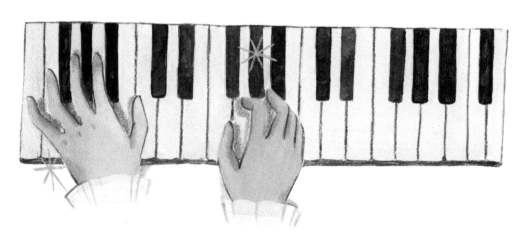

But his musical talent was about to be put to the test . . .

Ludwig began to lose his hearing, making him feel worried and sad—music was his life! Despite this, he kept working and created a piece called First Symphony. It was so full of energy that it left the audience amazed.

Next, Ludwig poured his sadness into one of his most beloved pieces, known as the Moonlight Sonata. It started as peaceful and calm as the night sky. But within the gentle music were gloomy notes that could make anyone feel quite blue.

Over the years, Ludwig used different tools to help him work. First, he tried a hearing trumpet to make sounds louder.

Later, as his deafness grew, he bit a pencil attached
to his piano to feel the vibration of the sounds.

Having almost completely lost his hearing, Ludwig felt angry and frustrated. But when asked to write his Ninth Symphony, he realized something incredible: he remembered the sound of every note and instrument.

Maybe Ludwig couldn't hear the music, but he could imagine it! He wanted this piece to take the audience on a journey from darkness to light. He decided it should end with a song inspired by a poem that celebrated humankind.

Everyone in Vienna was excited about the opening night. It was the first time a symphony had included a choir, as well as the largest orchestra ever put together. At the end, Ludwig couldn't hear the long applause. But he felt it in his heart.

And so little Ludwig—the great Beethoven—turned his feelings into music that still moves people today. He showed that joy, sadness, and everything in between can shine through melodies that come from deep within.

LUDWIG VAN BEETHOVEN

(Born 1770 – Died 1827)

1903

c. 1800s

Ludwig van Beethoven was born in Bonn, Germany. He grew up in a
musical family. His grandfather, who Ludwig was named after, was an
important conductor, meaning that he directed groups of musicians.
From an early age, Ludwig showed signs that he was a gifted piano player.
His father made him practice over and over, wanting Ludwig to be seen
as a talented child in the same way that a famous composer called
Wolfgang Amadeus Mozart had, just a few years before. Although Ludwig
played in public during his childhood, it was as he grew up that he
became known in Germany for his abilities on the piano. As a teen,
Ludwig actually visited Vienna, Austria, hoping to study with the great
Mozart, but had to return home because his mom was sick. When Ludwig

1814

1820

eventually moved to Vienna five years later, the city became his home. There, he played music and became a famous composer, writing pieces for every instrument in the orchestra. Over time, Ludwig lost a large amount of his hearing. Even when his hearing loss became stronger, he kept making music by remembering sounds and notes that he could no longer hear. He eventually retired from performing in public, and focused on being a composer. Ludwig wrote some of the most loved classical music of all time, changing the genre with his ideas. For example, he included a choir in a symphony, which had never been done before. His powerful music expressed emotions with a force and energy that, to this day, delights listeners around the world.

Want to read more about classical music?
Have a look at this great book:
Little People, BIG DREAMS: Mozart by Maria Isabel Sánchez Vegara
With the help of an adult, you can also listen to some of Ludwig's music online.

Text © 2025 Maria Isabel Sánchez Vegara. Illustrations © 2025 Romina Galotta.
Original idea of the series by Maria Isabel Sánchez Vegara, published by Alba Editorial, S.L.U.
"Little People, BIG DREAMS" and "Pequeña & Grande" are trademarks of
Alba Editorial, S.L.U. and/or Beautifool Couple S.L.
First published in the US in 2025 by Frances Lincoln Children's Books, an imprint of The Quarto Group.
Quarto Boston North Shore, 100 Cummings Center, Suite 265D, Beverly, MA 01915, USA
Tel: +1 978-282-9590 **www.Quarto.com**
EEA Representation, WTS Tax d.o.o., Žanova ulica 3, 4000 Kranj, Slovenia.

This book is not authorized, licensed, or approved by the estate of Ludwig van Beethoven.
Any faults are the publisher's who will be happy to rectify for future printings.
A CIP record for this book is available from the Library of Congress.
ISBN 978-1-83600-815-6
Set in Futura BT.

Published by Peter Marley · Managing editorial by Izzie Hewitt
Designed by Sasha Moxon, Izzy Bowman, and Karissa Santos
Edited by Lucy Menzies
Production by Robin Boothroyd
Manufactured in Guangdong, China CC052025
1 3 5 7 9 8 6 4 2

Photographic acknowledgements (pages 28–29, from left to right): 1. Portrait of German composer
Ludwig van Beethoven, after a painting by Christian Horneman, 1803. (Photo by Hulton Archive/Getty Images)
2. German composer Ludwig van Beethoven. Drawn by the artist Borckmann. (Photo by Rischgitz/Getty Images)
3. Ludwig van Beethoven, German composer. Crayon drawing by Louis Letronne. (Photo by Hulton Archive/Getty Images)
4. German composer Ludwig van Beethoven composing the 'Missa Solemnis', February—April, 1820.
Oil painting by August Klober. (Photo by Universal History Archive/Getty Images)

Collect the *Little People*, **BIG DREAMS**™ series:

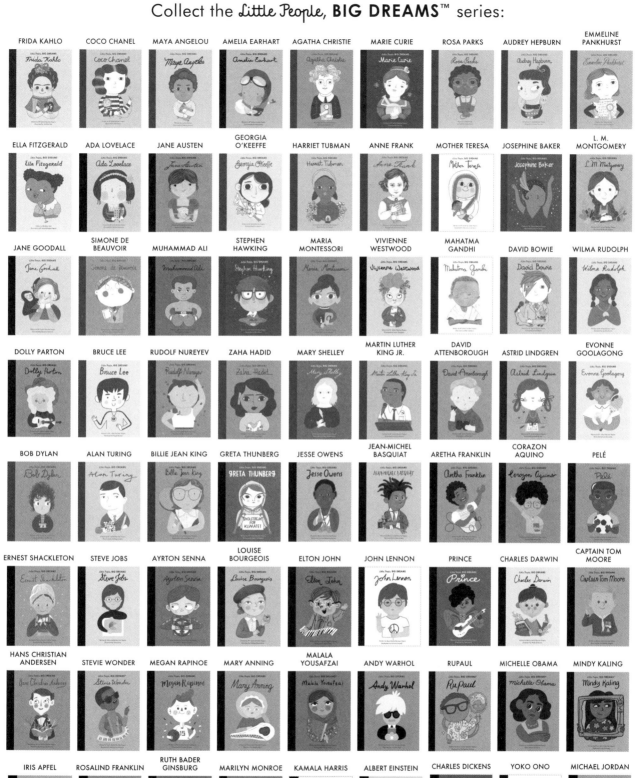

FRIDA KAHLO	COCO CHANEL	MAYA ANGELOU	AMELIA EARHART	AGATHA CHRISTIE	MARIE CURIE	ROSA PARKS	AUDREY HEPBURN	EMMELINE PANKHURST
ELLA FITZGERALD	ADA LOVELACE	JANE AUSTEN	GEORGIA O'KEEFFE	HARRIET TUBMAN	ANNE FRANK	MOTHER TERESA	JOSEPHINE BAKER	L. M. MONTGOMERY
JANE GOODALL	SIMONE DE BEAUVOIR	MUHAMMAD ALI	STEPHEN HAWKING	MARIA MONTESSORI	VIVIENNE WESTWOOD	MAHATMA GANDHI	DAVID BOWIE	WILMA RUDOLPH
DOLLY PARTON	BRUCE LEE	RUDOLF NUREYEV	ZAHA HADID	MARY SHELLEY	MARTIN LUTHER KING JR.	DAVID ATTENBOROUGH	ASTRID LINDGREN	EVONNE GOOLAGONG
BOB DYLAN	ALAN TURING	BILLIE JEAN KING	GRETA THUNBERG	JESSE OWENS	JEAN-MICHEL BASQUIAT	ARETHA FRANKLIN	CORAZON AQUINO	PELÉ
ERNEST SHACKLETON	STEVE JOBS	AYRTON SENNA	LOUISE BOURGEOIS	ELTON JOHN	JOHN LENNON	PRINCE	CHARLES DARWIN	CAPTAIN TOM MOORE
HANS CHRISTIAN ANDERSEN	STEVIE WONDER	MEGAN RAPINOE	MARY ANNING	MALALA YOUSAFZAI	ANDY WARHOL	RUPAUL	MICHELLE OBAMA	MINDY KALING
IRIS APFEL	ROSALIND FRANKLIN	RUTH BADER GINSBURG	MARILYN MONROE	KAMALA HARRIS	ALBERT EINSTEIN	CHARLES DICKENS	YOKO ONO	MICHAEL JORDAN

NELSON MANDELA PABLO PICASSO AMANDA GORMAN GLORIA STEINEM FLORENCE NIGHTINGALE HARRY HOUDINI J.R.R. TOLKIEN ELVIS PRESLEY NEIL ARMSTRONG

ALEXANDER VON HUMBOLDT NIKOLA TESLA WILMA MANKILLER MARCUS RASHFORD LAVERNE COX MAE JEMISON DWAYNE JOHNSON HELEN KELLER ANNA PAVLOVA

QUEEN ELIZABETH TERRY FOX HEDY LAMARR SHAKIRA FREDDIE MERCURY LEWIS HAMILTON LOUIS PASTEUR PRINCESS DIANA DAVID HOCKNEY

VANESSA NAKATE OLIVE MORRIS KING CHARLES MOZART STEVE IRWIN JÜRGEN KLOPP LEO MESSI SALLY RIDE TENZING NORGAY

KYLIE MINOGUE BEYONCÉ TAYLOR SWIFT RAFA NADAL USAIN BOLT SIMONE BILES STAN LEE LEONARD COHEN VINCENT VAN GOGH

MARY KOM SALVADOR DALÍ ANTOINE DE SAINT-EXUPÉRY DAVID BECKHAM KATHERINE JOHNSON PATRICK MAHOMES

YAYOI KUSAMA ROALD DAHL HARRY STYLES WILLIAM KAMKWAMBA MARY EARPS YVES SAINT LAURENT

BOB MARLEY VIRGINIA WOOLF LUDWIG VAN BEETHOVEN LOUIS BRAILLE

Scan the QR code for free activity sheets, teachers' notes and more information about the series at www.littlepeoplebigdreams.com